B51 075 735 2

KT-144-953

THE STORY BEHIND

SALT

Heidi Moore

www.raintreepublishers.co.uk
Visit our website to find out
more information about
Raintree books.

To order:
☎ Phone 0845 6044371
🖨 Fax +44 (0) 1865 312263
✉ Email myorders@capstonepub.co.uk

Customers from outside the UK please telephone +44 1865 312262

Raintree is an imprint of Capstone Global Library Limited,
a company incorporated in England and Wales having its
registered office at 7 Pilgrim Street, London, EC4V 6LB
– Registered company number: 6695582

"Raintree" is a registered trademark of Pearson Education
Limited, under licence to Capstone Global Library
Limited.

Text © Capstone Global Library Limited 2009
First published in hardback in 2009
Paperback edition first published in 2010
The moral rights of the proprietor have been asserted.

All rights reserved. No part of this publication may be
reproduced in any form or by any means (including
photocopying or storing it in any medium by electronic
means and whether or not transiently or incidentally to
some other use of this publication) without the written
permission of the copyright owner, except in accordance
with the provisions of the Copyright, Designs and Patents
Act 1988 or under the terms of a licence issued by the
Copyright Licensing Agency, Saffron House, 6–10 Kirby
Street, London EC1N 8TS (www.cla.co.uk). Applications
for the copyright owner's written permission should be
addressed to the publisher.

Edited by Louise Galpine, David Andrews,
  and Laura Knowles
Designed by Philippa Jenkins and Artistix
Original illustrations © Capstone Global Library Ltd
Illustrated by Gary Slater/Specs Art
Picture research by Mica Brancic and Elaine Willis
Originated by Modern Age Repro House Ltd.
Printed in China by CTPS

ISBN 978 0 431114 95 8 (hardback)
13 12 11 10 09
10 9 8 7 6 5 4 3 2 1

ISBN 978 0 431115 09 2 (paperback)
14 13 12 11 10
10 9 8 7 6 5 4 3 2 1

British Library Cataloguing in Publication Data
Moore, Heidi
The story behind salt. – (True stories)
553.6'32
A full catalogue record for this book is available from the
British Library.

Acknowledgements
We would like to thank the following for permission to
reproduce photographs: © AKG-images p. 25; Alamy pp.
iii (© Jupiter Images/Comstock Images), 13; Ancient Art &
Architecture Collection Ltd p. 22 (© R Sheridan); Corbis
pp. 18 (© Wolfgang Kaehler), 9 (© NASA), 16 (© Tim
Tadder), 26 (© Adam/photocuisine); Getty Images pp. 5, 7
(© Michael Rosenfeld), 14 (© Mark Joseph), 19 (© Jo-Ann
Richards), 20 (© AFP); iStockphoto p. 8 (© rotofrank);
Photolibrary.com pp. 4, 11, 15 (Stock RF/©Panorama
Media), 21; Shutterstock p. 17 (© Maxim Godkin); ©
The Bridgeman Art Library pp. 23, 24 (© Peter Newark
American Pictures/Private Collection).

Cover photograph of a Koli working in the salt marsh of
the Rann of Kutch reproduced with permission of Corbis
(© Frédéric Soltan/Sygma/Corbis).

Every effort has been made to contact copyright holders of
any material reproduced in this book. Any omissions will
be rectified in subsequent printings if notice is given to the
publisher.

All the Internet addresses (URLs) given in this book were
valid at the time of going to press. However, due to the
dynamic nature of the Internet, some addresses may have
changed, or sites may have changed or ceased to exist since
publication. While the author and publishers regret any
inconvenience this may cause readers, no responsibility for
any such changes can be accepted by either the author or
the publishers.

ROTHERHAM LIBRARY SERVICE	
B515735	
Bertrams	24/02/2011
JN	£6.99
BSU	J553.632

Contents

Some words are shown in bold, **like this**.
You can find out what they mean by looking in the glossary.

Salt from Earth

▲ **Whether very coarse or finely ground, salt has many different uses.**

Today, most people think of salt as something that makes food taste better. But it is so much more! Salt has hundreds of uses. It can be used for making ice cream, removing spots on clothes, and keeping cut flowers fresh. It can be used for treating sore throats, melting ice on roads, and making soap. Humans need salt to live.

This simple substance has played a large role in human history. The salt **trade** led to the growth of many cities and countries. Salt has been a factor in wars. It even helped start a **revolution**! It inspired people to overthrow a ruler.

This is the true story behind salt. Let's take a taste . . .

Salt tales ✔

In an old folktale, a king asks his three daughters to tell him how much they love him. The first two daughters tell their father they love him more than the finest things in the land. The third tells her father, "I love you like salt." This angers the king, and he forces her to leave the kingdom. Later his cook serves him a meal without salt. The meal is tasteless, and the king cannot stand it. Suddenly he realises the true value of salt and understands how much his daughter loves him. To be loved like salt was, in fact, a great compliment!

▼ **This Japanese sumo wrestler is tossing salt for good luck before a match.**

What is salt?

This photo has been magnified many times to show the shape of the salt crystals.

There are many types of salt. Most of the time, when people talk about salt, they mean table salt. The scientific name for table salt is sodium chloride.

By itself, **sodium** is a metal that explodes when it comes in contact with moisture. Chlorine on its own is a poisonous gas. But when they combine, they form a substance that both humans and animals need to live – salt.

Salt is also a **mineral**. Minerals are found in nature. A mineral is a solid substance that is made up of many **crystals**. Crystals are made up of tiny parts arranged in an ordered, repeating pattern.

Types of salt

There are two main types of salt.

Sea salt

Sea salt is found in sea water. Crystals of salt form when the sea water evaporates. Sea salt can have fine or **coarse** (rough) grains. It often contains small amounts of other minerals.

Rock salt

Rock salt is found in the ground. Another name for this form of salt is halite. Halite can be found in beds of minerals from **evaporated** (dried up) seas and lakes. It is purer than sea salt.

In the Bible ✔

When people say someone is "the salt of the earth", it means he or she is a good, honest person. The saying comes from a passage in the Bible.

◀ **Table salt is used to flavour food.**

Sea salt

▲ Sea water gets some of its salt from the rocks that are very slowly worn away by the ocean.

Have you ever wondered what makes the ocean salty? The salt comes from things that have **dissolved**, or broken down, in the water. Some of these things are rocks, **minerals**, and dead fish. Rain also washes some salt from the land into the ocean. The level of saltiness of a body of water is called its salinity. This is a measure of the amount of salt per volume of water. The ocean is 3.4 to 3.7 per cent salt.

Fresh water contains far less salt than salt water. Fresh water is what you find in most lakes and rivers. When 0.03 cubic metre (1 cubic foot) of sea water **evaporates**, it leaves 1 kilogram (2.2 pounds) of salt. However, 0.03 cubic metre (1 cubic foot) of water from a freshwater lake, such as Lake Windermere, contains only about 5 grams (0.17 ounce) of salt.

Salty planet ✔

Sea water covers more than 70 per cent of Earth's surface. Imagine that you could spread all the salt in the world's oceans across Earth's surface. It would form a layer more than 152.4 metres (500 feet) thick. That is about the height of a 40-story building!

◀ The Great Lakes in the United States, including the finger-shaped Lake Michigan, are freshwater lakes. They do not contain much salt.

Fancy sea salt ✔

Today, fancy, rare sea salts are prized for cooking. Hawaiian alaea sea salt gets its pink colour from red clay. Cyprus flake salt has unique, pyramid-shaped **crystals**. Some sea salts are smoked, to add extra flavour to dishes. Some of the top restaurants in the world serve these costly sea salts in dishes.

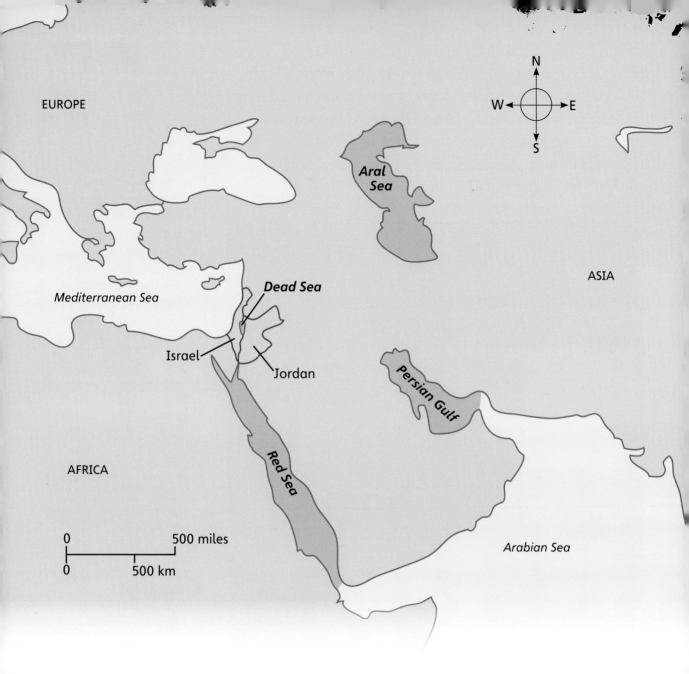

EUROPE

N

W E

S

Aral Sea

ASIA

Mediterranean Sea

Dead Sea

Israel

Jordan

Persian Gulf

AFRICA

Red Sea

| 0 | 500 miles |

| 0 | 500 km |

Arabian Sea

▲ Earth's four saltiest bodies of water are shown on this map as darker blue areas.

Not a drop to drink

Most sea water contains between 2.5 per cent and 3.5 per cent salt. The saltiest water is in the Dead Sea. This sea is on the border of the countries of Israel and Jordan (see map). It contains about 33 per cent salt. The Dead Sea is so salty that fish cannot survive in its waters. The next saltiest bodies of water are the Aral Sea, which contains about 10 per cent salt, the Red Sea, and the Persian Gulf. These each contain about 4 per cent salt.

It is not safe to drink sea water. If you were to drink it, your kidneys would take in far more salt than they could let out. Over time, if you did not take in any fresh water, you would die. So, always bring enough fresh water with you to the beach!

Good for floating

One thing salt water is good for is floating. The salt in sea water helps keep swimmers afloat. That is because sea water is denser (thicker) than fresh water. It pushes people up to the surface.

▼ **These swimmers float easily in the salty water of the Dead Sea.**

Water, water everywhere ✔

English poet Samuel Taylor Coleridge wrote a famous poem called "The Rime of the Ancient Mariner". A line in the poem says, "Water, water, every where, nor any drop to drink." The poem is about a fisherman stuck at sea. Even though water is all around him, he has nothing to drink.

Rock salt

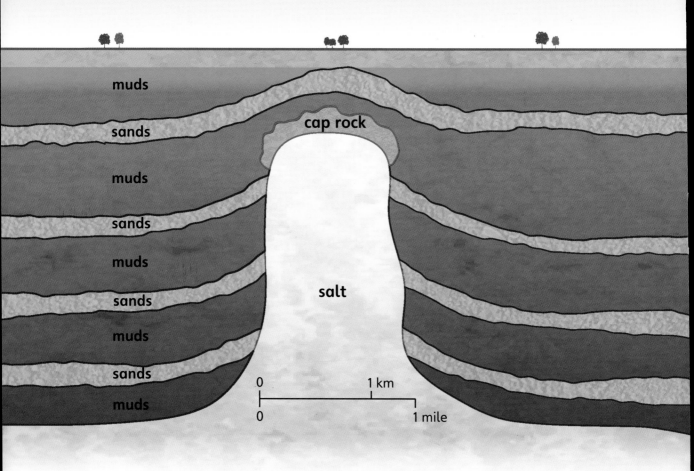

muds

sands

muds

sands

muds

sands

muds

sands

muds

cap rock

salt

0   1 km

0   1 mile

▲ **This is a diagram of a salt dome. The salt was pushed up through layers of mud and sand until it became blocked by the cap rock.**

Rock salt collects in beds (the bottoms) of **evaporated** lakes and oceans. There are beds like this all across the world.

Rock salt also can occur in large mounds known as salt domes (see diagram). These form when pressure from deep inside Earth pushes up large **deposits** of rock salt. Salt domes can measure about 1.6 kilometres (1 mile) across. Large salt domes can be found in Germany and along the Gulf Coast of the United States. A small salt dome is called a salt pillow.

People get rock salt from these salt domes by **mining**. They also get it by drilling down into the ground and using water to **dissolve** the salt. A salty liquid, called **brine**, then gets pumped to the surface.

City of salt ✔

About 335 metres (1,100 feet) under the city of Detroit, Michigan, USA, there is a huge salt cave. The huge salt mine takes up more than 607 hectares (1,500 acres). It has been a working salt mine for more than 100 years. Each year it supplies tens of thousands of tonnes of salt for de-icing roads. In some places the salt is over 122 metres (400 feet) thick.

Below the Detroit salt mine are many other giant salt deposits. Some experts think there might be about 27,215 trillion tonnes of salt in the area. That is enough to supply the entire world with salt for many years!

▼ Modern salt mines, such as this mine in Italy, use massive machines to remove rock salt.

Salt and ice

Rock salt is **coarser** than sea salt. It is not used for cooking as often as sea salt is. But it has some important uses. Rock salt is used to melt ice and snow on roads and to make things.

Pavement salt

If you live somewhere with cold winters, you have probably seen people putting salt on the pavements or roads. They do this when the roads and pavements are snowy or icy. The salt helps melt the snow and ice.

▶ **This truck is spreading salt on a slippery road to make it safer to drive and walk on.**

How does this work? Salt water freezes at a colder temperature than fresh water. Fresh water freezes at 0°C (32°F). Sea water freezes at -2.2°C (28°F). So, adding salt to the ice lowers its freezing point. This makes the ice melt and keeps it from freezing again. This makes streets and pavements safer – no slipping and sliding!

We all scream for . . . rock salt?

Rock salt was once used to make ice cream. Before refrigeration, an old-fashioned ice cream maker used a hand crank and ice cubes to make ice cream.

But the ice cream mixture freezes at a colder temperature than water. So, ice on its own could not freeze ice cream. It would not make the mixture cold enough. Adding rock salt to the melting ice creates a very cold mixture that is far colder than plain ice. The very cold salt water helps the ice cream mix to freeze. Soon you have ice cream!

▶ Before refrigerators were invented, salt was used to make ice cream.

Salt and the human body

▲ Salt is released from your body when you sweat during exercise.

The human body needs salt to function. Without salt, the **cells** in your body would die. Salt acts as an electrolyte in the body. Electrolytes are chemicals that help conduct (carry) electric charges to different parts of the body. These charges send messages that tell the cells what to do. They tell the lung cells to help you breathe and the muscle cells to move your body. They also help control your **blood pressure**.

The human body does not make salt. Humans must get it from the foods they eat. When a person takes in too much salt, the body releases it through fluids. If you have ever tasted your tears, you know that they taste salty. You might have noticed the same thing when licking your upper lip on a hot day. That is because tears and sweat both contain salt. Urine (liquid waste) also contains salt.

Today, most people do not need to worry about not getting enough salt. Most people get far too much (see page 27).

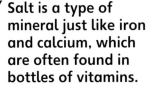

How much salt? ✔

An adult human body contains about 250 grams (8.8 ounces) of salt. That is enough to fill three or four saltshakers!

Minerals ✔

People take in many different **minerals**, such as iron and calcium. Do those minerals sound familiar? They might, if you have ever read the label on a bottle of vitamins. Iron and calcium are just two of the minerals people need to live.

▼ Salt is a type of mineral just like iron and calcium, which are often found in bottles of vitamins.

Salt rituals

▲ **In Russia, bread and salt are traditional gifts for visitors.**

Salt has played a role in many rituals around the world. In France and Germany, salt once had an important part in weddings. The bride and groom carried salt as a symbol of fertility. Fertility is the ability to have children.

In other countries, people bring salt to a new home. They believe it brings good luck to the people who live there. In Japan, salt is used to purify homes and other places. Many people in Japan believe salt will cleanse the home and rid it of evil spirits.

Sometimes people toss salt over their shoulder after spilling some. This is meant to ward off bad luck. This idea might have come from the fact that salt has long been considered important. People probably viewed spilling salt as very unlucky or careless.

Spa time!

Today, salt is often part of a different ritual. People use it at bath time! Many believe that salt is good for the skin. They add sea salts to bathwater. It softens the water and makes the skin feel silky smooth. Others scrub their bodies with salt to remove dead skin.

▼ Some people add salt to bath water for a healthy, soothing bath.

Blast from the past ✔

About 2,000 years ago, the Roman **historian** Flavius Josephus wrote about the health benefits of Dead Sea salt. He wrote, "The Dead Sea cannot be praised too highly. Travellers take this salt home because it heals the human body and is used in many medicines."

Salt throughout history

▲ Salt pan workers in Mumbai, India, gather salt by dragging it with rakes.

Salt has long been a part of people's lives. Scientists have found **saltworks** dating from thousands of years ago. Saltworks are places where salt is taken from the ground. One of the earliest was found in China. It was in use 8,000 years ago.

Saltworks were very important throughout history. Whoever controlled the salt had a steady supply for people and animals. Sometimes people went to battle for control of saltworks.

6000 BCE

Workers gather salt at the Shanxi saltworks in China. A method of dragging and gathering salt from the surface of a body of water is in use. A method of collecting ocean water in pots and boiling them is in use.

Early salt gathering

One early method of collecting salt was dragging and gathering. First, people would let the sun heat up a lake or other body of water. This caused salt **crystals** to form on the surface. Then people dragged pots across the surface to gather the salt.

Another method was to collect ocean water in clay pots and set them over a fire. The fire would boil off the water until only salt was left in the pot. A third method was to drill a well to collect salt from below ground. The well collected **brine** (salt water). It was called a brine well.

▼ Salt is an important part of animals' diets. These rams are licking salt they have found on a manmade road.

Follow the leader ✔

Millions of years ago, the earliest humans would find salt by following animals. They followed them to salt licks, brine springs, or other sources of salt. A salt lick is a salty spot in the ground that animals lick. The first roads humans built were on animal paths to salt licks and other sources of salt.

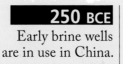

250 BCE
Early brine wells are in use in China.

Salt in ancient Egypt

Salt was an important part of life in ancient Egypt. The people in Egypt made salt by **evaporating** sea water from the Nile Delta.

The Egyptians used salt to make a substance called natron. They called it divine salt. They used natron to preserve the bodies of pharaohs (leaders) as mummies! Scientists have also found wooden containers of table salt in tombs (graves) in Egypt.

The people in Egypt also might have been the first people to **cure** meat and fish with salt. Curing is a way to preserve food. Salt keeps food from spoiling. It does this by drawing out water and killing bacteria (germs) in the meat and fish.

▶ **This Egyptian tomb painting from around 1400 BCE shows a woman carrying salt and bread.**

2000–1000 BCE
The ancient Egyptians use salt to cure meat and fish and to preserve bodies as mummies.

This 14th century painting from Italy shows a stall selling salt. Salt is so precious that it is sometimes called white gold.

Salt in ancient Rome

Salt also played a large role in ancient Rome. The Roman people built their cities near saltworks. The first great Roman road was the *Via Salaria*, or "Salt Road". It was used to carry salt across the Roman Empire (all the lands they ruled).

Salt sayings ✔

When people say something is "worth its salt", that means it is worth the cost. The phrase comes from ancient Rome. Soldiers there were often paid in salt. The word *salary*, meaning "pay", comes from this practice. Romans also called people in love *salax*, meaning "salted". The Romans had many terms connected with salt. This shows that salt was an important part of everyday Roman life.

27 BCE–476 CE
The Roman Empire develops. Cities were often built close to saltworks.

1000 BCE   500 BCE   0   500 CE

Salt today

Today, salt is more plentiful than ever. Within the past 200 years, people have found vast salt **deposits**. But that does not mean salt has become less valuable.

Salt and the US Civil War

Salt had a role in the US Civil War. This was a war between the northern and southern states between 1861 and 1865. At the time, salt was used to dye cloth, to preserve meat, and to make leather.

The South did not produce as much salt as the North. This gave the North an advantage. Over time the North captured two important Southern saltworks. This helped the North win the war.

▼ **This painting shows a Civil War battle that took place in the southern US state of Georgia in 1864.**

1800s–present	20 December 1864	1 February 1865
Vast salt deposits are found around the world.	Soldiers from the North capture and destroy saltworks in Saltville, USA, during the US Civil War.	Northern navy destroys saltworks in St. Andrews Bay, Florida, USA.

1800

1850

Gandhi's salt march

In 1930 India was ruled by Great Britain. Britain placed a high tax (money paid to a government) on salt, and many Indians were upset. The Indian leader Mahatma Gandhi led followers 322 kilometres (200 miles) to **salt pans**. These are areas where saltwater dries up and leaves salt behind. He urged Indians to get their own salt and resist British rule. This act sent a powerful message and helped inspire a **revolution**. India gained independence from Great Britain. Today, salt remains a symbol of freedom in India.

Salt's dark side ✔

With such high demand for salt, there is a need for workers to gather it. **Mining** for salt can be hard, dangerous work. At different times, prisoners have been forced to work in salt mines. The African slave **trade** is also linked to salt production. Many Africans were forced to work in salt mines in the United States and other countries.

◀ Gandhi leads his followers to the salt pans in his famous salt march.

1930
Indian leader Mahatma Gandhi guides followers to salt pans as a peaceful act against British rulers.

The future of salt

For such a simple substance, salt has had an amazing history. It has been used as money, to preserve bodies in Egypt, and to keep meat and fish safe before refrigeration. But today, the biggest issue is how salt affects health.

Dangers of too much salt

Doctors say people should not have more than 2.5 grams of **sodium** per day. That is about 6 grams, or one teaspoon, of salt. In the United Kingdom, most people have between one and a half and two teaspoons per day. That is too much! The human body only needs about one-quarter of a teaspoon per day.

Too much salt makes the body hold in more fluid. This forces the heart to work harder than it should to pump the fluid around the body. This can lead to heart disease. People with high **blood pressure** need to be extra careful about salt intake.

Cutting down on salt

You and your family can cut down on salt by using spices and fresh herbs instead of salt. Staying away from processed, or prepared, food also helps. Processed foods such as chips, cold meats, and canned goods are often very high in salt, and so is fast food. A typical fast food cheeseburger has over half a teaspoon of salt. That is more than half the salt a person should have in an entire day!

Still, salt has an important place at the table. It makes good food taste even better. You can still enjoy salt on your food. Just remember not to overdo it!

◀ **Cooking with fresh herbs is a healthy way to cut back on salt.**

Timeline
(These dates are often approximations.)

7000 BCE

2000–1000 BCE
The ancient Egyptians use salt to **cure** meat and fish and to preserve bodies as mummies.

1000 BCE

2000 BCE

250 BCE
Early **brine** wells are in use in China.

27 BCE–476 CE
The Roman Empire develops.

1st century
Roman **historian** Flavius Josephus writes about the health benefits of salt.

0

1798
English poet Samuel Taylor Coleridge writes "The Rime of the Ancient Mariner", with the famous line "Water, water, every where, nor any drop to drink."

1775

1750

1800s–present
Vast salt deposits are found around the world.

1800

1825

1975

1950

late 1990s/2000s
Doctors tell people to consume less salt; there are concerns over too much salt in people's diets.

2000

This symbol shows where there is a change of scale in the timeline, or where a long period of time with no noted events has been left out.

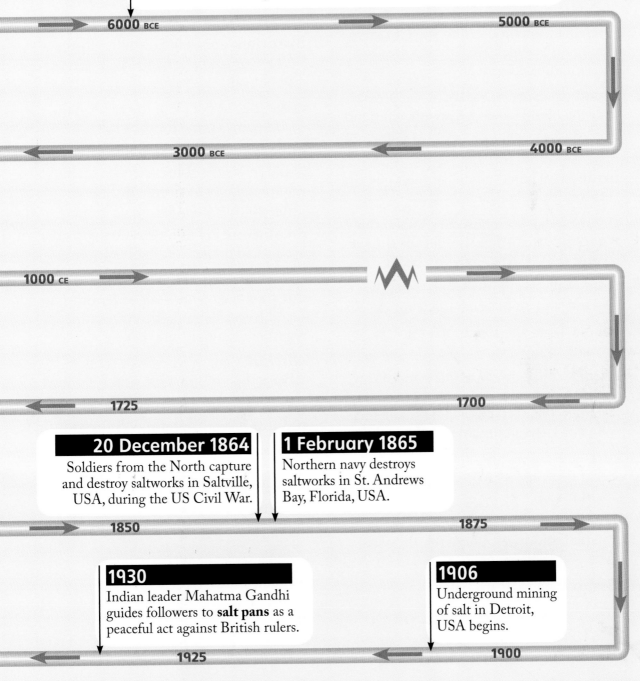

6000 BCE

Workers gather salt at the Shanxi **saltworks** in China. A method of dragging and gathering salt from the surface of a body of water is in use. A method of collecting ocean water in pots and boiling them is in use.

6000 BCE 5000 BCE

3000 BCE 4000 BCE

1000 CE

1725 1700

20 December 1864

Soldiers from the North capture and destroy saltworks in Saltville, USA, during the US Civil War.

1 February 1865

Northern navy destroys saltworks in St. Andrews Bay, Florida, USA.

1850 1875

1930

Indian leader Mahatma Gandhi guides followers to **salt pans** as a peaceful act against British rulers.

1906

Underground mining of salt in Detroit, USA begins.

1925 1900

Glossary

BCE meaning "before the common era". When this appears after a date, it refers to the time before the Christian religion began. BCE dates are always counted backwards.

blood pressure measure of the pressure of the blood passing through veins and arteries. A diet high in salt is dangerous for people with high blood pressure.

brine salty liquid. Some animals get salt from drinking brine.

CE meaning "common era". When this appears after a date, it refers to the time after the Christian religion began.

cell smallest unit in a living thing. All plants and animals are made up of cells.

coarse large and rough. Sea salt has coarse grains.

crystal solid substance made up of tiny parts arranged in an ordered, repeating pattern. Salt crystals can be small and fine or large and rough.

cure keep something from spoiling. Salt has long been used to cure meat and fish.

deposit build-up of substances by natural processes. Large salt deposits are good sources of salt.

dissolve break apart. Salt dissolves easily in water.

evaporate dry up. When sea water evaporates, it leaves behind salt.

historian person who studies history. The Roman historian Flavius wrote about salt.

mine dig or get from the earth. Salt companies mine for rock salt.

mineral solid substance found in nature and made up of many crystals. The human body needs many different minerals to function.

revolution act of overthrowing a ruler. Salt had a role in India's revolution against Great Britain.

salt pan area where salt water dries up and leaves behind salt. Ancient peoples gathered salt at salt pans.

saltworks place where salt is taken from the ground. One of the earliest saltworks was in use 8,000 years ago.

sodium type of metal. When sodium and chlorine combine they form salt.

trade act of buying or selling goods. The salt trade has been around for thousands of years.

Find out more

Books

The Rock We Eat: Salt, Laura Layton Strom (Children's Press, 2007)

The Story of Salt, Mark Kurlansky (G. P. Putnam's Sons, 2006)

Websites

Learn some interesting facts about salt!
http://www.saltsense.co.uk/aboutsalt-facts01.htm

This web page tells about the earliest production of salt that has ever been found.
http://www.sciencenewsforkids.org/articles/20050831/Note2.asp

Read about a "natural mummy." This 2,000-year-old body was found preserved in the Chehrabad salt mine in Iran.
http://news.nationalgeographic.com/news/2007/07/070703-salt-man.html

Place to visit

The Salt Museum
162 London Road
Northwich
CW9 8AB
www.saltmuseum.org.uk

Visit the Salt Museum, which is the only place in the UK where salt is produced on a large scale.

Index